FEEDING *Family,* FEEDING *America*®

EASY, FOOLPROOF RECIPES FROM OUR FAMILY TO YOURS

Allison Hill + MAINE SQUAD | Photography by Cristina Hill

PROCEEDS ARE DONATED TO THE NON-PROFIT HUNGER RELIEF ORGANIZATION, FEEDING AMERICA.

Published by Seacoast Press, an imprint of MindStir Media, LLC
1931 Woodbury Ave. #182 | Portsmouth, New Hampshire 03801 | USA
1.800.767.0531 | www.seacoastpress.com

Printed in the United States of America
Paperback ISBN: 978-1-7358186-8-9
Hardcover ISBN: 978-1-7358186-9-6

We take life one claw at a time. Ogunquit, Maine.

For all of the kind-hearted people out there...

You make the world a better place with all you do. Thank you for buying this book and helping to feed our fellow brothers and sisters.

Book collaboration with our extended family, affectionately known as "Maine Squad"

Ghirardini Family (Dave, Suzanne, Carlisle, Cate, Caroline)

Satter Family (Joan & Bob aka Noni & Pop)

Michelle McGann and Jonathan Satter (aka Auntie Michelle and Unky Monkey)

And...the Hill Family
Geoff, Chauncey, Cristina and me

Book Design by Exponent Collaborative and Unit B Creative

Introduction

Being busy can take its toll on small but special family moments that make life feel bigger, richer, and better. Homework, after-school activities, sports practice, dual-careers, caretaking – it all eats into our quality time, doing things we love with the people we love. That's why, when the girls were little, I started figuring out how to create super tasty meals which were easy and foolproof to enjoy as a family or with friends, or even a house crowded full of guests. Otherwise, I'd have to rush in from work each night and figure out how to make all the food groups in record time while gulping down a much-needed glass of wine. We learned that even when meal preparation is crazy, it's worth it once we gather around the meal and the sharing begins.

Then the pandemic hit.

I hopped in the car with my husband, two teenage daughters, and three dogs to drive sixteen hours straight from Atlanta to a small town in Maine called Ogunquit. It's a quiet little coastal spot with a permanent population of only 892. My parents met there on the beach one summer in high school, and it's been our summer vacation getaway ever since. Seemed like the perfect place to get away from the crazy for a bit.

Once we settled in, we started our quarantine routine of spending dinners – heck, every family meal – together. It became a precious time for us to enjoy each other's company. We kept the meals simple like we did any other busy day so we had extra time for card games, puzzles, and movie nights so that our quarantine time wasn't just all work and no play. As the disappointments of canceled sports seasons, canceled graduation, canceled summer jobs and three quarantine birthdays rolled by, it became abundantly clear this was the new normal... at least, for a while.

But as we watched the news, we soon noticed many people weren't as fortunate as we were. We had jobs that let us work from home, our girls had computers and Internet connectivity to do their school work, and we had food on our table. That food gave us our cherished family meal time. Many people didn't have any of these things. Even worse, the pandemic shone a bright light on the root causes of hunger in our nation, the structural and systemic inequities that disproportionately impact marginalized communities.

Things were so bad for so many families. The pandemic wreaked havoc on people, especially on children and seniors, due to no fault of their own. The extended effects will be tremendous. What could we do to help?

We decided to create a cookbook of our favorite quarantine meals to benefit those most in need, donating proceeds to Feeding America, the nation's largest and most effective organization that looks at the complex, root problems of hunger.

This book is meant to give ideas for creating delicious, flavorful foods that take very little effort and the whole family loves. They are beautiful, scalable, perfect for families of all ages, and use many 'normal' pantry ingredients. We also wanted the recipes to be foolproof so that even a beginner could make these dishes without worrying about a mismeasurement here or there. With our stay in Southern Maine, the book also includes the influence of one of the town's best, local ingredients we could pick up straight from the fishing boats on the dock – lobster!

It wouldn't be a family cookbook without the whole family participating. Our quaran-team grew, with my nieces and parents joining us and everyone joining in as key grips and food stylists. My daughter Cristina, age 16, was food photographer. My daughter Chauncey, age 19, was an incredible editor with a designer's eye. My super creative niece Carlisle was given the title Chief Naming Officer and my other nieces Cate and Caroline have an incredible eye for styling food. Of course, everyone's favorite role was taste tester. My mom edited until she couldn't take it anymore...lots of laughs in that process! Each night, we tasted, made dishes look delicious, and took photos. We soon realized how much fun this was too – something we could all participate in together as a family.

We were also determined to see this project through since we loved its purpose even more.

So, back to our original question: What could we do? Well, this – with the hope that our one family can do some good. Feeding our family, and in turn feeding America, with up to 100 meals donated for each book purchased.

We hope you enjoy the meals and this peek at our family.

xo,
Ali – (& team!)

"What you do makes a difference, and you have to decide what kind of difference you want to make."

- Jane Goodall

Hunger in America

Hunger is not a new issue for America but the COVID-19 pandemic has exacerbated this problem. Due to the effects of the pandemic, *more than 50 million people may experience food insecurity in 2020*, including a potential 17 million children. In a country that wastes billions of pounds of food each year, it's almost shocking that anyone in America goes hungry. Yet, there are millions of children and adults who do not get the meals they need to thrive. The Feeding America® network provides nourishing food – from farmers, manufacturers, and retailers – to people in need. At the same time, they also seek to help the people they serve to build a path to a brighter, food-secure future.

Feeding America is a nationwide network of 200 food banks and 60,000 food pantries and meal programs that provides food and services to people in need. They are the nation's largest domestic hunger-relief organization and helps 1 in 7 Americans. 1 in 7 of our neighbors is too many...but, the Feeding America network helps people live more food secure and stable lives. By supporting them and purchasing this book, you are joining efforts to help provide food to people in your community since their network food banks operate in all 50 states, Washington D.C., and Puerto Rico.

Contents

Rise and Shine

Auntie Michelle's PB Toast

Lobster Scramble

Breakfast in Bread

Lazy Day Egg Casserole

Whole World in Your Ham

Just What the Dr. Ordered Pancakes

Sunshine Yogurt Bowls

Oh so simple, this toast has so much flavor when the bread and spread is warmed up together (versus regular toasting and then spreading). Other topping favorites include local honey, granola, banana, and thin slices of apple. There are so many delicious 'butters' on the market today too – use your favorite nut or seed butter like almond or sunflower – although we prefer straight-up peanut butter.

Auntie Michelle's PB Toast

When there is a big crowd at the house all waking up at various times, this is a great dish that looks beautiful stacked up on a plate and is a complete meal served with a big bowl of mixed fruit. Easy. This super casual dish is perfect for making sure no one is 'hangry' starting off their day. It is also a really fun thing to serve when kids are around to decorate faces and make sure they start the day right with a healthy breakfast. We like the hearty multi-grain bread and of course, fresh blueberries. Our yard in Maine has tons of wild blueberries that start ripening in mid-July so we find ourselves putting blueberries on almost everything around that time.

INGREDIENTS

Favorite Bread Slice
Peanut Butter
Mixed Fruit & Nut Mix
Blueberries

INSTRUCTIONS

Heat oven to 350 degrees. Spread a heavy amount of peanut butter or your favorite type of spread on the bread slice. Bake for 5 minutes to let the peanut butter get hot and gooey. Sprinkle the chopped fruit and nut mix and fresh fruit.

The Palm Beach Post | November 11, 2

'I am a
DIABETES
WARRIOR

Auntie Michelle, also known as LPGA star Michelle McGann, knows the importance of a healthy, protein-filled breakfast. As a professional athlete with Type 1 diabetes, she has dedicated her energy to her foundation that educates kids on how to live a long and healthy life with this disease.

Lobster for breakfast? Yes, please. This is especially a hit with company who don't expect such a decadent way to serve scrambled eggs. If you don't have lobster, the lump crabmeat from the grocery store does just as well in the decadence department.

Lobster Scramble

What to do with leftover lobster? This breakfast recipe is the perfect solution. So creamy, delicious and it elevates a simple breakfast to a whole new level of elegance. The creaminess of the cheeses really complements the lobster but any 'white' cheese works well (don't ruin the look with your shredded cheddar please!). If you don't have any leftover lobster, head to Perkins Cove and visit Heidi and Jeb at Cove Café. Hands down the best breakfast in Ogunquit...or, make that the world! The Lobster Frittata is a must.

INGREDIENTS

½ pound lobster

6 eggs

¼ cup butter

1 heaping teaspoon stone ground mustard

1 Tablespoon cream (heavy or light)

1 oz brie

1 oz Parmesan

   Chopped parsley and/or chives

Serves 4

INSTRUCTIONS

Crack eggs in a mixing bowl. Add cream and mustard and whisk until creamy and smooth.

Melt butter in pan and add lobster so the lobster gets nice and buttery. Try not to eat the lobster out of the pan. Add eggs and sprinkle small pieces of brie and Parmesan over top. I use the shaved Parmesan in the container. Gently fold the eggs to incorporate the cheese by moving your spatula under and then turning over. Be careful not to overmix or overcook the eggs so they stay creamy.

Serve with sprinkled parsley or chives. *Voila!* Gourmet eggs in under 5 minutes.

This is a hit even with people who think they don't like eggs. The best thing is that the presentation comes out perfectly every time no matter if the eggs are over-easy, over-medium, or even over-hard.

Breakfast in Bread

This became a family favorite in part because it looks so cute. We love serving hot breakfast items like this with a simple arugula salad. We toss the arugula in a bit of olive oil, salt, pepper and squeeze of lemon. Another tip – cook your bacon in the oven instead of the stove top. Saves lots of greasy mess and the bacon comes out perfectly crisp every time. We bake at 350 degrees for 25 minutes or until cooked between the perfect amount of floppy and crisp. Make sure to garnish your eggs with the pepper, too... It tastes great but also elevates the look to pro status.

INGREDIENTS

1 thick slice of sourdough bread per serving
1 egg per serving
   Pat of butter

INSTRUCTIONS

Melt a pat of butter in a saute pan over medium heat. Cut a hole in the center of the bread. Saute bread on both sides in the butter so there is crispiness on both sides. Crack an egg in the center and let cook for 4-5 minutes depending upon how you like your egg. Our family taste testers think it is best after 4 minutes and a little runny so it soaks into the bread. The sourdough taste gives it a nice contrast to the creaminess of the egg.

Garnish with freshly ground black pepper.

This casserole is a foolproof method to serve a delicious breakfast or brunch to a crowd. I love serving with a simple salad – mixed greens dressed with olive oil, squeeze of lemon, balsamic vinegar, salt, and pepper. Any bread flavor can be used but we voted that sourdough brings the best flavor.

Lazy Day Egg Casserole

INGREDIENTS

4   or so bread slices

4   mini sweet peppers (varying colors)

12 baby sweet tomatoes - 6 red, 6 yellow cut in 1/2

1   12-oz. package of shredded Italian cheese

½   cup light cream

1   heaping tablespoon grainy Dijon mustard

2   apple sausage links

10 Mozzarella pearls

¼   cup butter, cut into little pieces

10 eggs

    Salt & Pepper to taste

Serves 8

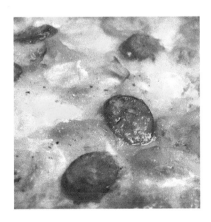

Not sure if it is done? Using a toothpick, poke the center of the casserole. If the toothpick comes out clean, it is ready to go!

INSTRUCTIONS

Place bread in a casserole dish, layering the bottom. The bread does not have to cover the whole bottom. Sprinkle Italian cheese, tomatoes, peppers over top creating a vibrant layer of colors. Pour ¼ cup of light cream evenly over top, to soak the bread overnight (or at least a couple hours). You can tilt the casserole dish back and forth to distribute evenly.

When ready to bake, whip together the eggs and remaining ¼ cup of light cream, along with the Dijon mustard. Dot the top of the casserole with small pieces of butter. Pour the egg mixture evenly over the top. Cut the apple sausage on a bias in 1/8 inch slices (prettier look) and randomly distribute over the top. Then, dot the top with 10-12 mini mozzarella pearls.

Bake for 1 hour at 350 degrees until the eggs cook through and a knife comes out clean in the center. Let sit for 10 minutes covered in foil before cutting into generous squares.

*You can also place your other favorite items at the base
of the ham before you crack the egg - goat cheese, diced
peppers, diced baby tomatoes, caramelized onions.*

Whole World in Your Ham

I used to call these 'ham cups' until the Maine Squad told me that was the worst name ever. So, we voted and my niece Carlisle came up with this new name (and many others in the book). Such a great name because it reminds me of a sunrise... when you really feel like you have the whole world in your hands. This is a great dish for a crowd – again, the presentation works for itself, eggs can be cooked to any temperature. This is another breakfast we like with salad. This time, served with spinach with just a touch of squeezed lemon, salt, and pepper.

INGREDIENTS

2   thick slices of ham per serving

1   egg per serving

   Parmesan cheese, shredded

Serves 1; Multiply as needed

INSTRUCTIONS

Heat oven to 350 degrees. Place two slices of ham inside a muffin tin. Make sure these are thicker slices so the ends curl and caramelize but don't burn. Sprinkle Parmesan cheese inside the base of the ham cup.

Crack an egg inside. Bake for 12 minutes for a gooey delicious egg - longer if you prefer over hard.

Garnish with freshly ground black pepper.

One sunrise on Ogunquit Beach and you'll never question the universe again.

The batter is so delicious, be aware that you will have many wanting to lick the bowl! Top with butter and local maple syrup to taste. Great for helping with a hangover. (See Perk Me Up Bloody Mary too on page 94 for a complete mental re-set morning).

24

Just What the Doctor Ordered Pancakes

INGREDIENTS

2 cups flour

2 Tablespoons granulated sugar

4 Tablespoons Dr. Pepper soda

1⅓ cup milk

2 Tablespoons cinnamon sugar

2 teaspoons vanilla extract

2 teaspoons salt

4 teaspoons baking powder

2 eggs

   Powdered sugar for garnish

   Berries for garnish

   Butter

Serves 8

INSTRUCTIONS

Combine all ingredients in a mixing bowl until fully incorporated and there are no lumps of flour. Heat a frying pan over medium-low heat with a pat of butter. When the butter melts, add 1/3 cup of batter in small circles or whatever size pancake you desire.

Flip the pancake once you see small bubbles appear in the batter. Cook for another minute or so once flipped and then remove. They will thicken and puff up once flipped.

Be careful to not put the temperature too high or the butter will burn. Add more butter in between batches.

When a magazine was doing a shoot at our house, I invited the photographers and stylists to stay with us. Then, I thought... oh no, now I have to feed them and they look healthy! This dish ended up being a hit... a beautiful, simple way to feed everyone a healthy breakfast before their run. They loved it!

Sunshine Yogurt Bowls

Another simple assembly that packs a powerful punch of flavors. This is also fun for kids of all ages by setting up a breakfast bar for guests to choose their own toppings.

INGREDIENTS

Greek Yogurt
Granola
Blueberries, Strawberries, Pomegranate Seeds
Local Honey

INSTRUCTIONS

We like using non-fat, unflavored yogurt so the local honey and sweetness of the fruit can take center stage. Spoon yogurt into a pretty bowl and top with your favorite toppings.

Power Lunches

Greens and Grains

Nana's Chicken Salad

Filet Mignon Soup

Avocado Panzella Salad

Best Turkey Sandwich Ever

Dave's Wicked Good Clam Chowdah

Old-Fashioned Lobstah Roll

White Chili

We used our side dishes from the night before to create this hearty, nutritious salad. With plenty of carbs and super foods, it is filling and energizing for a day of fun. Other vegetables that are delicious are radish, squash, and zucchini. Have fun experimenting. The dressing is light and ties all the flavors together nicely.

Greens & Grains Salad

INGREDIENTS

6 cups mixed lettuce
1 cup pumpkin, cubed
1 cup red bell pepper, chopped
1 cup cooked cous cous, rice or grain
   Pumpkin seeds

Buttermilk Dressing:

1 cup buttermilk
¼ cup mayonnaise
¼ cup apple cider vinegar
¼ cup white wine vinegar
1 teaspoon salt & freshly ground pepper

Serves 8

INSTRUCTIONS

Heat oven to 400 degrees. Place cubed pumpkin and peppers on a sheet pan. Grocery stores make this type of recipe super easy by doing the work for you – just pick up the containers of cubed vegetables they have already chopped. Toss with avocado oil, salt, and freshly ground pepper. Bake for 30 minutes until golden, soft and caramelized. Let cool for 10 minutes.

Plate lettuce, add grains, pumpkin, peppers and pumpkin seeds. Combine dressing ingredients and whisk together. Dress salad as you see fit.

Every time we roll into Nashville to visit my husband's family, my mother-in-law Anna always has a big batch of chicken salad waiting for us. She makes hers with more mayonnaise and as a 'farmer's daughter' swears that is the best way. And, of course, she is right! It is a terrific staple to feed a crowd and can be created so many different ways.

Nana's Chicken Salad

Recipe by Anna Hill

INGREDIENTS

2¼ pounds chicken breast

²/₃ cup light mayonnaise

2 stalks celery, chopped small

1 small sweet onion, chopped small

Salt & freshly ground pepper

Serves 8

INSTRUCTIONS

Boil chicken for 20 minutes. Let cool. Rough chop the chicken (smaller for sandwiches and larger chunks for salad). Add celery, onion and mayonnaise and then combine. Add salt and pepper to taste. We make this as the base recipe and then add varying flavor profiles like chopped dill and diced green grapes or curry and chopped almonds. This version is more on the dry side, but of course, add more mayo if you like a creamier texture.

This base chicken salad recipe can be changed up so many ways. For a fresh, summer taste try 1 Tablespoon chopped dill and a squeeze of ½ lemon. For a bolder taste, try a ½ cup of sliced grapes, ½ cup of chopped almonds and ¾ teaspoon of curry. Yum, yum.

A light broth with hearty ingredients makes for a fulfilling lunch. Serve with your favorite crunchy bread for dipping... The second day is even more flavorful than the first. Also serves as a perfect dinner. We used leftover broccoli instead of corn for this batch.

Filet Mignon Soup

Sometimes I look in my refrigerator, scratching my head over what to do with all of the delicious leftovers that no one wants to eat. Especially on a night when everyone is moving in different directions, I can find myself miscalculating and having more leftovers than usual. One of these nights was when I had beautiful, delicious, perfectly cooked filet mignon (see page 64) looking at me on a chilly spring day. It seemed like a perfect plan to make a decadent soup.
The beauty of this recipe is that you can truly throw in any leftover protein, vegetables, or starch and the flavors will blend together to create a rich-tasting meal that gives the taste of having spent hours and hours perfecting it.

WHATEVER YOU HAVE

12 ounces leftover filet mignon, cut into bite size cubes
12 fingerling potatoes, quartered
1   sweet onion, diced
1   Tablespoon garlic
12 oz frozen corn
12 oz frozen peas

SOUP BASE

48 oz chicken stock
24 oz crushed tomatoes
1/4 cup red wine
2   dashes of apple cider vinegar
1   tsp salt freshly ground pepper
1/2 tsp basil   1/4 Tbsp butter
1/2 tsp garlic salt   1/4 cup cream
1/2 tsp chili flakes   1/4 cup grated Parmesan

INSTRUCTIONS

Saute onions in butter until transparent and slightly caramelized. Add garlic and saute one minute, being careful not to burn the garlic. Add all the remaining ingredients except for the cream and Parmesan cheese and set on medium heat until soup begins to bubble, around 20 minutes. Turn down heat to low and simmer to let the flavors come together and do their magic for another 40 minutes - although sometimes hungry people come by the pot and dig in earlier. Stir in cream and Parmesan cheese during the last 5 minutes of cooking. No exact science is necessary, so it is fine to fix it and forget it. The longer the flavors blend, the tastier it is! Top with a sprinkle of shredded asiago cheese and a thick slice of crusty bread. Filet is best based on its tenderness. (Filet recipe is on page 64.)

Geoff's Menu Hack: Put this marinade/vinaigrette on everything and anything – including, the base chicken salad, street taco slaw and leftover fingerling potatoes. Chicken, shrimp, fish do very well with this marinade, too.

36

AVOCADO VINAIGRETTE

You can reserve the marinade from the shrimp appetizer on page 59 after draining or make a fresh recipe by whisking together the ingredients below.

MIX TOGETHER:

1 cup vegetable oil or avocado oil

1 cup wine vinegar

½ cup lemon juice

Juice of 1 orange

1 Tablespoon Dijon mustard

1 avocado cut into small pieces

1 Tablespoon salt

¼ tsp black pepper

2 tsp sugar

1 tsp dried thyme

1 tsp dried mustard

2 tsp dried oregano

½ tsp garlic powder

Extra recipe:
Cook salmon enclosed in foil on a hot grill with sliced lemons, capers, sliced onions and 2 Tablespoons of vinaigrette. We cook ours on high but indirect on the upper rack for 15 minutes.

Avocado Panzella Salad

INGREDIENTS

4 bread slices, cubed

2 hothouse cucumbers

2 avocados

1/2 small red onion, cut in thin half moons

2 tomatoes, cut in wedges

Serves 8

INSTRUCTIONS

Toast bread cubes in 400 degree oven for 5 minutes. Toss bread, cucumbers, avocados and red onion together with ½ cup of the Avocado Marinade from the Avocado Shrimp Appetizer.

Creamy, gooey and yummy is how to describe this hearty sandwich. Putting a light layer of the cream sauce on the outside creates a crusty, flavorful outside to the bread, too. Serve with a light salad or our favorite – the crunch of BBQ Cape Cod chips.

Best Turkey Sandwich Ever

Caramelized onions are delicious on so many things, we like to make a big batch at the beginning of the week to add to recipes. Cut onions to desired shape – half moons, diced – and then saute in butter, salt and pepper until translucent and slightly browned. If you aren't up for making the world's best sandwich at home, check out Cornerstone in the heart of Ogunquit. It features the best artisanal pizza and mouth-watering sandwiches. They also own the next door Village Food Market, the amazing butcher counter and grocer.

INGREDIENTS

½ cup sour cream

1 heaping Tablespoon horseradish
Multi-grain bread slices

½ pound turkey, sliced medium

8 slices of cooked bacon

8 slices creamy white cheddar cheese

1 cup caramelized onions

1 pat butter

Serves 4

INSTRUCTIONS

Mix sour cream and horseradish in a small bowl. Do a taste test and make sure it has a little kick. Once it is combined with the other ingredients, it will lose its punch a bit. Spread a light layer on both sides of the bread. Yes, that is not a typo. It is amazing how crunchy, crispy and yummy the bread will be. Melt a pat of butter in a frying pan over medium-low heat. Once the butter is melted, toast the bread for a minute on each side. Build your sandwich on both sides. Add 1 cheese slice per bread piece and then top one side with two slices of turkey and the other side with two slices of bacon and a spoonful of caramelized onions. Put a cover over top for a couple minutes and let all the ingredients get gooey with the cheese melting and warm throughout. Take cover off, put the two pieces of the sandwich together and continue cooking until brown and golden on both sides. Even my daughter who hates onions, was surprised how much she loved this!

Growing up with my cousin David was always entertaining and now he wows me with his amazing cooking. This chowder recipe is decadently rich and thick with lots of shortcuts for flavor to make it easy. Even better, his incredible three daughters helped out with the cookbook and have such big hearts for all humankind.

40

Dave's Wicked Good Clam Chowdah

Recipe by David Ghirardini

The Evans Family has been creating chowder goodness for over 40 years in their famous restaurant, The Lobster Shack, at the edge of Perkins Cove. A cup of chowdah, a cold draft beer — you just entered New England heaven. Beers allowed when making this at home.

INGREDIENTS

 6 slices of bacon (diced)

1½ cups chopped onions

 1 cup chopped celery

 2 10-ounce cans of baby clams or minced clams

 2 14-ounce cans of diced potatoes

 4 sprigs fresh thyme

 1 (10.75-ounce) can condensed cream of celery soup

1 (10.75-ounce) can condensed cream of potato soup

1 quart half-and-half cream

1 pint heavy whipping cream

1 (8-ounce) package of Philadelphia Cream Cheese

Salt, pepper, garlic powder (to taste)

Oyster Crackers

Serves 8

INSTRUCTIONS

Place the bacon in a large pot and cook over medium-high heat, stirring occasionally, until crisped and browned, about 10 minutes. Remove the bacon with a slotted spoon, leaving the drippings in the pot. Set the bacon aside. Stir the onions and the celery into the bacon fat. Season with salt, pepper, garlic powder, and cook for 5 minutes, stirring frequently. Mix cream of celery soup, cream of potato soup, 1 can undrained clams, 1 can drained clams, half-and-half cream, and whipping cream into the pot. Add thyme.

Cut the Philadelphia Cream Cheese into cubes and add to pot. Add cans of potatoes (drained). Add half of the bacon. Cook and stir on medium to medium-low heat until ingredients meld together. Taste to see if more spice is needed. Let simmer for another 15 minutes. Serve in bowls with remaining bacon pieces sprinkled on the top and of course, oyster crackers!

This roll takes an ordinary lunch to a whole new level. We love serving this when company visits for a quick lunch. Amazingly, you can't find split-top buns in the South! Crazy, right? We ship them in or if we are packing light (ha), put them in our luggage when we head back home to Atlanta.

Old Fashioned Lobstah Roll

The key to an amazing lobster roll is toasting the bun with melted butter. Brush melted butter on both sides of the bun and lightly cook in a pan. If you are like my dad, you may prefer a grilled bun.

INGREDIENTS

1 ¼ pounds of lobster meat, cut into chunks

½ cup light mayo

 1 lemon, squeezed

½ teaspoon celery salt

¼ teaspoon freshly ground pepper

¼ cup finely chopped celery

    Paprika

    Split-top buns

¼ cup butter

¼ small sweet onion, chopped

Serves 3-4

For our family picnic celebrations, like Fourth of July, we make a big batch that people can spoon onto a salad or put into a grilled, buttery roll. There is usually plenty left over to make Lobster Scramble eggs the next day too – or, our other favorite –an amazing over-the-top garnish for a Bloody Mary.

INSTRUCTIONS

Put onion and celery in a food processor and process to get it really fine. In a bowl, combine the cut lobster meat and melted butter, folding so each piece of lobster gets its fair share of goodness. Then, fold in mayonnaise, lemon juice, celery salt, and ground pepper until all combined.

Spoon into the warm, buttered bun and sprinkle with lots of paprika. If you want to be really authentic, serve with Ruffles and some sliced sweet pickles.

A musical of flavors, you just can't go wrong with white chicken chili. Healthy, full of flavor, your guests will be asking for seconds and thirds!

White Chicken Chili

INGREDIENTS

1   sweet onion, chopped
32 oz ground chicken or turkey
64 oz chicken broth
1   can of white beans, drained
2   cans white corn, drained
2   Tbsp each of brown sugar, mascarpone, light cream
1   green chili diced finely, seeds and ribs removed
    (optional for extra heat!)
1   batch of Allison's special seasoning (below)
    Cinnamon
1/4 cup pumpkin seeds
1   avocado
1/2 cup sour cream
1   Tbsp of chopped cilantro

Serves 10-12

INSTRUCTIONS

Using your soup stock pot, saute onion in a pat of butter and olive oil until almost translucent. Add chicken meat, folding into onions and stirring to separate meat so it doesn't chunk up. I usually break it up with a wooden spoon. Season meat with 1 tsp of Allison's special seasoning.

Cook chicken through and then let simmer on medium-low for 5-8 minutes to let meat absorb the flavors (just don't let it go too long or too high where it dries out). Add corn, beans, chicken broth, and remaining batch of Allison's special seasoning. Let simmer on medium for 20 minutes. Add brown sugar, mascarpone and light cream.

Serve garnished with a dollop of sour cream, cilantro, avocado, light sprinkle of cinnamon and pumpkin seeds.

ALLISON'S SEASONING:

1 Tablespoon salt	½ teaspoon:	¼ teaspoon:
½ teaspoon:	Chili powder	Garlic salt
Granulated onion	Cayenne pepper	Allspice
Ground cumin	Chili flakes	Freshly ground pepper

Make a bigger batch of this seasoning to keep it on hand for Bloody Mary's, grilled chicken rub or anything you can think of! We multiply by 10 and keep it in a small jar so it is available at a moment's notice.

Happy Hour Appetizers

Noni's Parmesan Asiago Dip

Maine-style Charcuterie Board

Maine Oysters

Caviar Dip

Steak Bruschetta

Shrimp, Avocado, Orange Faux Ceviche

Unky Monkey's Cheesy Crisps

This is literally cheese crack and everyone is so excited when Noni breaks this out for an appetizer. A creamy, yet peppery flavor profile, it works great on hearty crackers, bread or even mixed into a salad. This also freezes really well, so make a big batch and pull it out whenever the craving strikes.

Noni's Parmesan Asiago Dip

Recipe by Joan Satter

INGREDIENTS

½ pound Parmesan

½ pound Asiago

2 teaspoons minced garlic

2 teaspoons dried oregano

1 teaspoon red pepper flakes

2 Tablespoons chopped green onion

1½ cups extra virgin olive oil

1 teaspoon ground pepper

Serves 8

INSTRUCTIONS

Cut cheeses into 1-inch chunks with rinds removed. Place them in the food processor with pepper, oregano and garlic and pulse until reduced to small pieces. Add green onion, olive oil, black pepper, and pulse again. Garnish with parsley and serve with any type of tasty cracker or crostini.

No matter what part of the country you are in, the best way to put together a board is to source local ingredients... local cheeses, local meats and your local grocer can help point you in the right direction. Then just load it up in sections and it will look inviting and accessible. Don't be afraid to pile it up!

Maine-style Charcuterie Board

INGREDIENTS

Green grapes

Oysters

Local cheeses

Prosciutto and salami

Hot honey and fig jam

Almonds

Pickles

Olives

Crackers

Serves a crowd!

The girls love designing the board as much as they do eating it. Assemble with your favorite crackers, nuts and olives. We love using Silvery Moon Creamery Brie, Hatch Knoll Farm Cheddar and Fuzzy Udder goat cheese. You can't go wrong with freshly sourced cheese paired with a dot of hot honey or fig jam.

Love them or hate them, all have to agree that oysters are extremely healthy, rich in protein and antioxidants. The myth is also true. They are great for the libido with proven increases in testosterone after eating. More... please?!?

Maine Oysters with
Fresh Mignonette *Recipe by Geoff Hill*

MC's in Perkins Cove, named after owners Mark Gaier and Clark Frasier, truly has the best, freshest oysters... well, really the best everything with their extremely creative, delicious menu. A must-visit restaurant for any foodie, it has also been named for having one of the top restaurant views in the world.

INGREDIENTS

    Oysters, shucked by the seafood shop

    Lemons

1 Tablespoon red onion, finely diced

1 Tablespoon red wine vinegar

1 Tablespoon white wine vinegar

    Sugar, pinch

1 teaspoon kosher salt

INSTRUCTIONS

This mouthwatering oyster sauce has the perfect amount of acidity. Combine red onion, vinegars, salt, and sugar to make the mignonette sauce. Squeeze lemon over top, add sauce or cocktail sauce on top and slurp away.

It's really easy to shuck oysters if you have the right tool. If you want to attempt it on your own, we recommend watching a YouTube video or two that will show you exactly how it's done.

The best part about this beautiful appetizer is that the caviar can come right out of the jar. "Oh no," your snob friends say? Get new friends—they sound lame. This is delicious, creamy, decadent, and easy.

Caviar Dip

We've noticed that the more appetizers were served, the less we actually enjoyed the tastes of dinner. We changed that by serving lighter and smaller appetizers that just whet the appetite and help the first couple cocktails go down. Grocery store caviar works just fine but you can also amp it up with more expensive versions from your local grocer. When we are going fancy we love Beluga caviar from the Huso huso sturgeon. Still amazing, but less expensive, is the Regiis Ova. Caviar by Chef Thomas Keller

INGREDIENTS

1   cup sour cream
1   heaping tablespoon of caviar
    Vegetable chips

Serves 8

INSTRUCTIONS

Yup - that's it for the easiest elegant hors d'oeuvre ever. It is the perfect amount of salt and creaminess that goes perfectly with cocktail hour. The vibrant colors of the chips raise the presentation factor but are also the most delicious crisp and taste to complement the dip.

Another good one for your leftover filet. We like to cut the filet into small pieces so it is easier to take a bite. When you plate this up, be messy! It looks great when some of the pieces fall off and the balsamic splashes on the plate.

Steak Bruschetta

We did our best to copy the recipe from That Place, the go-to scene for cocktails, appetizers, more cocktails, then dinner, finished up with more cocktails. Owner, Rick Dolliver, is always there to welcome you with a smile.

INGREDIENTS

Baguette loaf, sliced (or your favorite hearty bread)

¼ cup Mascarpone cheese

½ cup Parmesan cheese, shaved

20 Baby red and yellow tomatoes, each sliced into 6 pieces

5 Basil leaves, rough chopped

Balsamic vinegar

Extra virgin olive oil

8 oz filet mignon (leftovers from page 64), cubed into the same size as tomato pieces

Salt

Freshly ground pepper

Serves 8

INSTRUCTIONS

Preheat oven to 350 degrees. Spread a thin layer of mascarpone cheese over bread and sprinkle a small amount of Parmesan evenly over top. Bake 4 minutes to warm up.

In a separate bowl, combine tomatoes, basil, balsamic vinegar, filet, olive oil, salt and pepper; let marinate together for a few minutes.

Remove bread from the oven and place onto your platter. Drizzle balsamic over each bread slice. Place tomato mixture on top and garnish with basil.

This can also be a delicious lunch salad served with endive or your favorite lettuce. I like the firmness and crispness of endive, along with its contrast of bitterness against the sweet of the orange.

AVOCADO VINAIGRETTE

Whisk together the ingredients below to create the marinade for the shrimp, onion, avocado, and oranges.

MIX TOGETHER:

1   cup vegetable oil or avocado oil
1   cup wine vinegar
½   cup lemon juice
    Juice of 1 orange
1   Tablespoon Dijon mustard
1   Tablespoon salt
¼   tsp black pepper
2   tsp sugar
1   tsp dried thyme
1   tsp dry mustard
2   tsp dried oregano
½   tsp garlic powder

Shrimp, Avocado, Orange Faux Ceviche

Recipe by Joan Satter

INGREDIENTS

2   pounds cooked shrimp, tails off
2   avocados, cut into chunks
1   small sweet onion, sliced thin
3   cuties or similar orange, peeled
    and divided into segments

Serves 8

INSTRUCTIONS

Place shrimp, avocado, onion and orange segments into marinade. I just use a large plastic bag. Marinate for at least 6 hours for all flavors to combine but ideally for 24 hours. Sometimes we add the shrimp for only the last hour so the marinade doesn't toughen it up. Drain and serve on a white platter to let the colors really pop. When draining, reserve the marinade to use as a dressing. That's what we used for the Avocado Panzella Salad and it is also great to marinate chicken for grilling.

Serve with toothpicks for easy eating.

*You will be surprised how
quickly these get eaten up!
Perfect combination of flavors.*

Unky Monkey's Cheesy Crisps

Recipe by Joan Satter

INGREDIENTS

1   cup shredded cheddar

1   cup cut bacon, raw

1   cup sweet white onion chunks

   Rye bread mini-toasts

Serves 8

INSTRUCTIONS

Combine cheese, bacon and onion in the food processor and pulse until an almost smooth texture.

Heat oven to 400 degrees. Spread cheese spread evenly over toasts. Bake on a cookie sheet for 20 minutes until cheese is bubbly and browned.

This is Unky Monkey...When he gave my daughter Chauncey a stuffed monkey for her third birthday, she immediately renamed him Unky Monkey and the name stuck! He and his wife, pro golfer Michelle McGann, were married in Ogunquit with all their cutie nieces as flower girls.

It's Dinner Time

Perfect Filet Mignon

"You're Roasted" Chicken

Lobster Boil

This Lasagna is the GOAT

Apple Sausage Pasta Night

Drunken Mussels

Apricot Mustard Chicken

Beach Day Ribeye

Street Tacos

Juicy Turkey Burgers

Our Favorite Oven Sides

Such a delicious filet needs some equally flavorful sides like a good ol' fashioned twice-baked potato and crisp asparagus.

Perfectly Cooked Filet Mignon

INGREDIENTS

4 pound filet, trimmed and tied

½ cup Dijon mustard

¼ cup Kosher salt

    Ground pepper

Serves 12

INSTRUCTIONS

Preheat oven to 500 degrees. Rub kosher salt and ground pepper onto meat, massaging gently. Then spread a thin layer of Dijon mustard over all sides. Cook for 25 minutes, testing with a meat thermometer for 125 degrees. Let rest under foil for 10 minutes.

LEMON DILL ASPARAGUS

A way to make any side vegetable taste fresh and more flavorful is to add a squeeze of ½ lemon and a favorite herb. For our asparagus, we sautéed 3 lbs of asparagus in butter and topped with ¼ cup chopped dill. Also, with asparagus, be careful not to overcook when sautéing. That means, take it off the heat right when it turns bright green. As it rests, it will continue cooking.

TWICE-BAKED POTATO

Wash 6 potatoes and prick with a fork. Brush olive oil and then roll in kosher salt. Bake for 1 hour at 350. Let cool.
Mix together 1 cup cottage cheese, 1 cup shredded cheddar cheese, ½ cup sour cream and the scooped out insides of potato halves sliced lengthwise. When scooping, leave enough potato around the outside to create a sturdy 'boat'. Fill with a heaping helping of the potato cheese mixture and bake for 30 minutes at 425 degrees or until you see them fully melted and crisping on top. Garnish with chopped chives. These potatoes are guaranteed to get your teenager to hug you.

Don't get caught up in the day and cocktails and forget that this chicken is 20 minutes per pound. Oh wait... that's me! Yes... a few nights, I've served dinner at 10:30 because I forgot to put the chicken in. It is so delicious but put it in early enough that your crowd doesn't get hangry. Trust me.

"You're Roasted" Chicken

INGREDIENTS

1   Roasting chicken
¼   cup brown sugar
2   Tablespoons honey
½   cup low-sodium soy sauce
2   oranges, juiced
½   stick of salted butter
2   Tablespoons minced garlic
1   teaspoon apple cider vinegar
1   sweet onion, chopped
1   Tablespoon orange zest
    Kosher salt
    Ground pepper

Serves 4-6

When cooking whole chickens, a 4 pound chicken can feed about 4-6 people. Let cool under foil for 10 minutes before slicing to let all the juices and marinade soak in.

INSTRUCTIONS

Pat chicken with paper towels until thoroughly dry, even drying inside the cavity (remove the neck, etc inside the cavity and discard). Cover with a generous amount of kosher salt, up to ½ cup, and massage in the skin. Prepare your basting marinade in a small pot. Saute diced onions in butter until cooked through and transparent. Add brown sugar, honey, soy sauce, orange juice, orange zest, garlic, apple cider vinegar.

Cook for 5 minutes over medium-low heat until sugar is fully dissolved. Let cool. Place chicken and marinade in a large plastic bag and marinate 6-8 hours.

Cook at 400 degrees, 20 minutes per pound. You can baste with extra marinade.

67

Lobster is such a fun dinner party food. It's messy, everyone looks silly in a bib. It's inevitable that a piece of shell flies across the room, and overall, it creates a warm, inviting ambiance full of laughs. Lobster, salad and maybe some corn... Everyone will be satisfied.

Lobster Boil

If we aren't eating at Barnacle Billy's – our absolute favorite restaurant in Ogunquit, Maine – we try to copy their salad recipe but never get it quite right. Tossed iceberg lettuce, sliced carrots, sliced red onion and Italian dressing mixed with paprika. We're still working on finding the secret dressing recipe. Anyone out there want to help?

INSTRUCTIONS

The secret of a really good lobster is using water from the sea. Yup – that's right! Send your kids down to the water with some buckets and have them fetch the seawater for the perfect boil and taste. If you don't have seawater within an arm's throw, use ¼ cup of kosher salt per gallon of water.

Put enough seawater in the pot - a 20-quart pot works well - so that the pot is about half full. Bring seawater to a boil. Leaving the claw ties on, put lobsters into the lobster pot head first and one at a time. Put on the lid and cook for 11-12 minutes - if your lobsters are over a pound and half or you have a very full pot of lobsters, add 2-4 minutes. The steaming leaves the lobster succulent and delicious.

Melt lots and lots of butter for dipping.

Serve one lobster per person with an individual small bowl of butter, crackers (as in shell crackers not eating crackers!), a small pick and lots of napkins.

Perkins Cove.

You really can't go wrong with lasagna, especially when you add goat cheese. The extra zip of the cheese plus the use of sausage instead of ground beef, makes it over-the- top delicious.

This Lasagna is the GOAT

Recipe by David Ghirardini

The name of this recipe has some funny history. My husband is a die-hard, emotional, unwavering Bills fan and has even hypnotized our two daughters into being the same. My side of the family grew up with the Patriots. Ooops. A little rivalry. My Patriots-loving cousin named his lasagna as a play off goat cheese but also a subtle dig at Geoff. Funny!

INGREDIENTS

1 pound mild Italian sausage

1 pound hot Italian sausage

½ onion, minced

2 cloves garlic, crushed or 1 heaping teaspoon minced garlic

1 (28-ounce) can crushed tomatoes

2 (6-ounce) cans tomato paste

2 (6.5-ounce) cans canned tomato sauce

½ cup red wine

1½ teaspoons dried basil leaves

½ teaspoon fennel seeds

1 teaspoon Italian seasoning

1½ teaspoons salt, divided, or to taste

¼ teaspoon ground black pepper

Red pepper flakes (to taste)

4 Tablespoons chopped fresh parsley

12 lasagna noodles

8 ounces ricotta cheese

8 ounces cottage cheese

8 ounces crumbled goat cheese

2 eggs

¾ pound fresh mozzarella cheese, shredded

¾ cup grated Parmesan cheese

2 Tablespoons red wine vinegar

Serves 8-10

INSTRUCTIONS

Boil noodles according to instructions on package and let cool. Spread a very thin layer of tomato sauce on bottom of a 11x13 casserole dish so the noodles don't dry out. Next, layer noodles over the sauce, slightly overlapping each noodle. If there are any open corners, simply cut one of the noodles to fit that space so there is a complete layer of pasta.

Next, spread about half of the soft cheese so it is an even, thin layer over the pasta.

Next, layer about half of your meat mixture evenly on top of the cheese.

Then, sprinkle shredded mozzarella or four cheese Italian blend over the meat.

Now repeat. Top with your next layer of noodles. Put the rest of the cheese mixture and the meat layer on top. Sprinkle with shredded cheese.

Place one more noodle layer on top. Spread a generous amount of red sauce over the top of the noodles. Cover completely with shredded cheese. Then, for the best part... For extra creaminess, take spoonful-sized amounts of fresh buffalo mozzarella and evenly space over the top. Sometimes we even use mozzarella pearls.

Bake for 1 hour at 350 degrees – you will be able to see the sauce bubbling and the cheese on top browned and gooey. Let it sit under foil for 15 minutes before serving. If it's too hot when cut, it will flop and fall apart. Garnish with fresh basil.

Serve with Italian salad and garlic bread. A winner on so many levels!

Meat Layer:

Cook sausages, onion, and garlic over medium heat until well browned. Stir in crushed tomatoes, tomato paste, tomato sauce. Season with basil, fennel seeds, Italian seasoning, 1 teaspoon salt, pepper, red pepper flakes and 2 tablespoons parsley. Add red wine and red wine vinegar. Simmer, covered, for at least 20 minutes but you can also let it go as long as 1 ½ hours if you get distracted. If you don't have all of these seasonings, just use what you have and honestly you can't go wrong with a little basil, little oregano. The secret is the red wine vinegar and red wine. It really elevates the taste.

Cheese Layer:

In a mixing bowl, combine cheeses (except shredded mozzarella and parm), eggs, remaining parsley, and 1/2 teaspoon salt.

Fresh herbs add so much flavor to any dish. You don't have to be a pro gardener to grow your own herbs. We just bought a nice cart on Amazon that we put outside the kitchen window. The herbs exploded in no time and make every meal so fresh tasting.

Apple Sausage Pasta Sauce

Surprisingly, this is always the pasta dish my girls ask me to make when their friends are coming over. So rich in flavor, it is the perfect complement to the homemade pasta. I always serve it alongside a Bolognese sauce so everyone can choose. My always-creative mom loves to mix them into one!

INGREDIENTS

3 apple sausage links, cut on the bias into small slices

1 package bella mushrooms

1 package white button mushrooms

   Olive oil

4 Tablespoons butter

½ cup cream

½ cup Parmesan or Italian blend shredded cheese

1 cup chicken broth

½ sweet onion, chopped

Serves 8-10

INSTRUCTIONS

Saute sausage over medium-low heat with olive oil for about 4 minutes until browned on both sides; deglaze pan with ½ cup chicken broth, gently stirring the bottom to lift up the sausage pieces. Add chopped onion and 2 Tbsp butter and cook another 5 minutes until onions are translucent. Add mushrooms, another ½ cup of chicken broth and continue cooking another 7 minutes until mushrooms are cooked. Stir in cream, rest of the butter and Parmesan.

Homemade Pasta Dough

One time making homemade pasta and you'll never want boxed pasta again. The dough can be made in a few easy steps and creating the pasta makes dinner a fun activity at the same time. Great for a Sunday early dinner and company and kids love to make it too. My husband Geoff started this tradition and we've never turned back!

INGREDIENTS

2 cups flour

3 eggs

1 teaspoon kosher salt

INSTRUCTIONS

1. Make a volcano. Slowly incorporate flour into the 3 eggs until wet and sticky.

2. Knead together until it forms into a dough ball and wrap in plastic wrap. No exact technique needed!

The word kneading means to work dough, usually by hand, for the purpose of developing the glutens in the flour, which is what gives baked goods their structure and texture.

MAKING THE PASTA

We use the Marcato brand pasta maker but there are several brands that work really well. Once the pasta rests on the drying rack for a few minutes, boil pasta in salted water with a touch of olive oil for two minutes. DO NOT RINSE your pasta with water once done.

A common mistake made that really affects flavor whether you are making homemade or boxed pasta is rinsing it with water. By not rinsing it, the starch stays and allows sauces to marry the pasta and create a more flavorful taste.

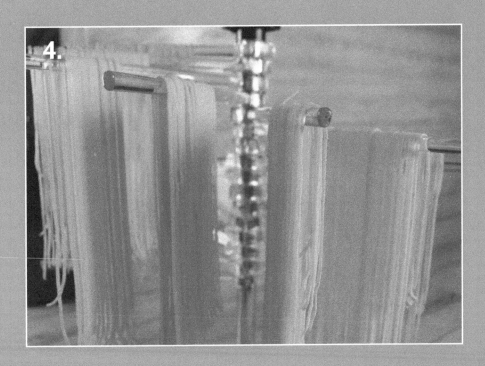

Mussels are always a crowd favorite with its rich bursts of flavor; be sure to stock up on lots of crusty bread for dipping into the delicious broth.

Drunken Mussels

INGREDIENTS

2   shallots, diced

2   cups chicken broth

1   cup sherry

1   cup white wine

½   cup bleu cheese crumbles

½   cup diced yellow tomatoes

2   teaspoon garlic salt

2   chorizo sausage links, sliced

4   Tablespoons butter

2   scallions, chopped (white and green)
    Parsley, chopped for garnish

2   pounds mussels

Serves 4

*I like to cut sausage
on the bias for a
prettier and more
elegant look.*

INSTRUCTIONS

Test mussel freshness by gently tapping each and ensuring they are tightly closed. Discard any that remain open. Cook diced shallots and sliced chorizo sausage in 4 tablespoons butter for approximately 2-3 minutes over medium heat until sausage is slightly browned.

Add 1 cup sherry to deglaze the pan for 2 minutes. Deglazing is just a way to bubble up all the delicious sausage bits on the pan and adds a dimension of flavor. Add chicken broth, white wine, yellow tomatoes, garlic salt and pepper. Cook for 5 minutes to blend flavors. Reduce heat to medium-low. Add mussels and steam for 5-6 minutes. Add bleu cheese and scallions, stirring gently.

Serve in a shallow bowl with lots of broth and crusty bread for dipping. Garnish with chopped parsley. Our favorite is traditional French bread.

Always so moist (no – Mom, don't use that word!) and tender, the chicken is really foolproof. Even if all you have is the apricot and mustard on a busy night, go for it! Guaranteed delicious.

Apricot Mustard Chicken

My niece likes to say – "How does this chicken stay so juicy?" – and the secret is baking it in the sauce. We like to serve this with an instant rice and Brussels sprouts. We substitute chicken broth for water when making the rice and then chop in fresh herbs for extra flavor. The Brussels sprouts are cut in half and then sautéed with chopped bacon, shallots, ¼ cup of chicken broth and a few dashes of low sodium soy. Cook without a cover (so they don't steam) until crispy outside and soft inside.

INGREDIENTS

8 chicken breasts, pounded flat

6 oz apricot preserves, ½ jar

2 Tablespoons grain mustard

½ teaspoon allspice

½ teaspoon granulated onion

1 small onion, chopped

   Creamy white cheddar cheese, 1 slice per chicken breast

   Salt & pepper

Serves 8

After you roll up the chicken breasts, put close together in the baking dish which will help them stay as juicy as possible.

INSTRUCTIONS

Preheat oven to 400 degrees.

Mix apricot preserves, mustard, allspice, granulated onion, and chopped onion. Lay chicken flat and tear cheese slices into smaller pieces, and lay across the breast. Cover with a heaping tablespoon of apricot sauce. Roll chicken breast tucking the ends under. Pour remaining sauce over top. Bake for 40 minutes. Serve one chicken breast per person.

This has been a hit from middle school through high school with all of my daughters' friends. The marinade does all the work for you and the meat truly melts in your mouth with the most delicious pop of flavor.

FINGERLING POTATOES

Cut into halves and combine with 2 tablespoons melted butter and a teaspoon of minced garlic. Bake at 375 degrees for 30 minutes and fork tender.

GRILLING PERFECTION

The sugar content of this marinade means cooking medium rare is the best flavor profile to caramelize but not overcook. Put grill on high and cook for 2 minutes on each side to sear meat. Move to indirect cooking – we place on an upper rack – turn grill to medium and cook another 6 minutes. Thick cuts work best.

Beach Day Ribeye

When grilling, we go for easy, low-maintenance sides so the focus can be on cooking the steak to perfection. Ribeye has the right fat content to offset the marinade – other cuts of meat would result in a very tough meat so stick with the ribeye. Also, only low-sodium soy sauce. You will ruin your steak if you use regular soy – the salt content is too high.

INGREDIENTS

4 thick ribeye steaks

2 cups low-sodium soy sauce

2 tablespoons apple cider vinegar

¼ cup brown sugar

6 ounces pineapple juice

1 teaspoon minced garlic

¼ teaspoon white pepper

¼ teaspoon granulated onion

Serves 8

INSTRUCTIONS

Combine all ingredients except for ribeyes in a saucepan. Cook over low heat until sugar is fully dissolved. Let cool and then marinate steaks. Using a large plastic bag works well so you can turn them every once in a while to make sure marinade penetrates on all sides. If pineapple juice isn't around, we substitute with orange juice. They will still be tasty after a 24-hour marinade but 48-hours is even better.

These street tacos are mouth-watering delicious and will surely be added into the rotation list. The marinated chicken can also be grilled or pan cooked without the bread crumbs. A crowd favorite!

Street Tacos

Tortilla Spread:

½ cup crème fraiche (or sour cream)

1 avocado, mashed

Slaw:

½ cup shredded carrots

½ cup baby cucumber, sliced and halved

½ cup sweet mini-peppers, sliced

½ cup white corn

2 tsp cilantro

6 Tablespoons of rice vinegar

Set aside and let marinate for best flavor combination)

Chicken:

4 thin chicken cutlets (or pound thin)

½ cup hoisin sauce

1 dash oyster sauce

2 tsp low-sodium soy sauce

1 egg

½ cup vegetable oil

1 cup panko bread crumbs

Mini-tortillas

Feta cheese (optional)

Serves 4

INSTRUCTIONS

Combine crème fraiche and mashed avocado. Set aside.

Combine vegetables, rice vinegar and cilantro. Set aside to marinate.

Combine hoisin sauce, oyster sauce, soy sauce and egg. Whip together. Put chicken in marinade to fully coat.

Dredge chicken in panko bread crumbs. Heat skillet with ¼ cup vegetable oil to medium-low heat. Keep it low so bread crumbs don't burn. Cook panko dredged chicken in pan —only turning once. 3 minutes on each side; over-turning will cause breading to fall off. It's really important for chicken to be pounded very thin.

Let chicken sit for 5 or more minutes before slicing into strips. If doing batches of chicken, place on a cookie sheet and keep warm in the oven at 225 degrees.

Place mini-tortillas in pan for about 1 minute on each side until they 'puff' up and become crispier.

Build tacos with crème fraiche spread, feta cheese crumbles, slaw and chicken. Delicious!

Street Corn:

Cook corn through. We simmer with the pan ¼ full of water where corn is not quite fully covered with the water. Add lid and steam for 10 minutes until bright yellow.

Roll corn in butter, use a light spread of the crème fraiche mixture and a sprinkle of Allison's Seasoning (page 45).

To make this a complete meal, serve with roasted carrots and a cucumber salad. Roast carrots, sprinkled with salt, in a 350-degree oven for 25 minutes. Toss sliced cucumbers in rice vinegar and dill.

Juicy Turkey Burgers

INGREDIENTS

1 pound of turkey, ground

¼ cup apricot preserves

½ cup chopped nut mix, chopped fine

½ cup crème fraiche (or sour cream)

½ cup bleu cheese crumbles

    Hawaiian rolls

    Butter lettuce leaves

    Tomato, thick slices

    Red onion, thinly sliced into rings

Serves 4

INSTRUCTIONS

Combine turkey, apricot and nut mixture. Form into turkey patties sized for your roll. We like to make slider size patties so we can eat two for dinner! Turkey burgers never work right on the grill no matter how hard we try (even with indirect heat). The best way is to pan cook them or cook them on a flat top if you have one. Heat to medium with a small amount of oil in the pan. Sear on both sides, about 2 minutes per side. Never push a patty down since you will release the juices, just let it do its thing! You can turn to low and finish cooking, or we like to put them in a 350 degree oven for another 6-7 minutes.

In a small bowl, melt the bleu cheese in the microwave for 40 seconds. Combine crème fraiche into bleu cheese.

When patties are done, let sit for 5 minutes so juices stay within. Assemble burger with the cheese/crème fraiche mixture on both sides of the bun, turkey burger, lettuce, onion, tomato. Voila! Juicy and flavorful.

With so many vegetables being sold in microwaveable packages, it really is easy to create a more robust vegetable flavor by doing a quick 2 minutes in the microwave and then finishing them off in the oven with various spices and flavors.

Our Favorite Oven Sides

INGREDIENTS

Potato, sliced thin

Parsley flakes

Green beans, trimmed

Lemon, juice of

Dill, chopped

Garlic salt

Cauliflower head, chopped

Paprika

Extra virgin olive oil

Salt and pepper

INSTRUCTIONS

Preheat oven to 400 degrees.

Cut cauliflower into small bite-size pieces, toss with olive oil and sprinkle with paprika, salt, and pepper and bake for 45 minutes.

Slice potatoes into thin slices, drizzle with olive oil, sprinkle with parsley flakes, salt, and pepper, and bake for 30 minutes.

Steam bag of green beans for two minutes in microwave, place on baking sheet and drizzle with butter. Bake for 10 minutes. Squeeze fresh lemon over top and sprinkle with chopped dill, salt, and pepper when serving.

Anytime Cocktails

Anyone who has spent at least a wee bit of time with us, knows we love our family cocktail hour. While everyone has their favorite go-to, these are a few cocktails we wanted to share.

Maine Mimosa

Blueberry Refresher

Bourbon Milk Punch

Ogunquit Punch

Perk Me Up Bloody

BLUEBERRY REFRESHER

1-2 jiggers vodka - *or 3 if your kids are being really loud*

 Lime, cut into wedges

 Mint

Fill glass with ice. Add vodka, squeeze of a fresh lime wedge, crushed mint leaves (crushing them slightly releases the aromatics). Then, top with ½ club soda, ½ flavored soda like San Pellegrino Arancia and one tablespoon of the Tree Tops Blueberry Syrup. So refreshing. Lovely afternoon cocktail with a hint of sweetness to contrast the peppery notes of Noni's Parmesan Dip.

MAINE MIMOSA

Tree Tops Blueberry Syrup:

1 cup blueberries

2 Tbsp simple syrup

2 Tbsp Chambord

Simmer until blueberries start to break down - about 5 minutes over medium-low heat

Squish with a fork to make a thick syrup; do not drain. While that cools, take a lemon wedge around the edge of the champagne glass and then dip in sugar to create a sugar rim

Place a small amount of syrup in the bottom of the champagne glass. Pour sparkling wine or champagne over top. Garnish with 3 blueberries floating. Perfect complement to the healthy sunshine yogurt bowl.

92

BOURBON MILK PUNCH

When our great friend and chef Dickie Brennan from New Orleans, recommended a delicious bourbon punch for our morning brunch, I cringed a little bit. One sip and I was hooked! Not only delicious, but it also guarantees the best mid-day nap.

We make a big pitcher and then pour over ice.

Per Serving:	Per Pitcher:
Jigger of bourbon	8 jiggers of bourbon
½ jigger of dark rum	4 jiggers of dark rum
2 ounces of milk	2 cups milk
¼ teaspoon vanilla extract	2 teaspoons vanilla extract
Fresh nutmeg, grated	

Mix and pour over ice. Serve with a sprinkle of fresh nutmeg.

OGUNQUIT PUNCH

Mix up a batch, invite your friends over and kick back on the porch. This is an Ogunquit favorite. Truth be told, I normally sneak this on to the beach, too. Shhhhhhh...

1 cup orange juice

1 cup pineapple juice

1 can flavored seltzer

½ cup light rum, Bacardi of course!

½ cup dark rum

1 Tablespoon cherry juice

   Freshly grated nutmeg

If at home and being civilized (versus teenager-like on the beach), garnish with wedges of fresh orange, maraschino cherries, fresh pineapple or whatever you have!
Of course, always feel free to add more rum to taste.

THE FLIBSIE

My mom's mom - known affectionately as Grammy to me - also had a nickname with her friends - Flibsie. We aren't sure how that nickname came to be but one thing we do know - Flibsie had tons of friends, loved to laugh and was always the life of the party. Her drink was clean, simple, elegant and suited her perfectly. Otherwise known as the Classic Martini and a favorite that seems to have been passed down.

Find the largest martini glass you have. Pour gin (or vodka) into a shaker.

Add ice. Stir gently. Forget the vermouth.

Pour into a chilled martini glass. Add olives. Get ready to laugh!

ALLISON'S SEASONING:

1   Tablespoon salt
½   teaspoon:
    Granulated onion
    Ground cumin
    Chili powder
    Cayenne pepper
    Chili flakes
¼   teaspoon:
    Garlic salt
    Allspice
    Freshly ground pepper

PERK ME UP BLOODY

INGREDIENTS

V8 or tomato juice

Pickle spear

Lemon wedge

Stuffed green olive

Beef jerky

Worcestershire sauce

Hot sauce

Vodka

Allison's Special Seasoning

INSTRUCTIONS

Put a generous serving of Allison's Seasoning on a plate and a generous serving of Worcestershire sauce on another. Dip your serving glass rim into Worcestershire sauce and then the seasoning to coat the rim with spicy goodness. Add your favorite vodka - 1 ounce if before 8 a.m. - 2 ounces if after. Then, add V8, 1 teaspoon of Allison's Seasoning and then the ice. You don't want the ice to melt into your vodka so add last. Garnish with celery stalk, lemon wedge (squeeze in lemon) and a skewer of cut pickles, olives and beef jerky. Add dashes of Worcestershire and hot sauce to taste. Perfect with the Lazy Day Casserole. When I was really trying to impress a friend this summer, I also added a huge piece of lobster to the skewer. I'm pretty sure that photo went viral.

Sweet Tooth

Auntie Jean's Kahlua Cake

Lil' Blueberry Angels

Mini Oreo Créme Pies

Whoopie Pies

Caramel Watermelon Ice Cream

Peanut Butter Banana Split Pudding

You can bring or serve delicious desserts without having to create everything from scratch. This Kahlua cake is a perfect example of adding just a couple ingredients and the flavor is out of this world.

Auntie Jean's Kahlua Cake

The first time I met my cousin's wife, she arrived with this amazing, decadent chocolate cake that I couldn't get enough of... moist, light, chocolatey but not heavy. It is so easy and so delicious, you won't believe it.

INGREDIENTS

1   15-oz package of your favorite chocolate cake mix

1   3-oz package of instant chocolate pudding

1   16-oz container of sour cream

¾   cup Kahlua

¾   cup vegetable oil

4   eggs

1   cup of chocolate chips

1   teaspoon cinnamon

   Powdered sugar, for garnish

INSTRUCTIONS

Preheat oven to 325 degrees.

Mix all the ingredients in a bowl, stirring in chocolate chips last. Pour into a greased (sprayed with Pam) bundt cake pan. Bake for 50 - 60 minutes. You can check with a toothpick once done (comes out clean). Let cool. Then flip onto your serving plate and sift powdered sugar over top. We garnished ours with some fresh mint on the side. So pretty!

This blueberry reduction is great to make in larger batches to use for pancakes, yogurt toppings and our favorite, a way to up the ante on a vodka & soda. Even more decadent, is a teaspoon in your favorite champagne or sparkling wine as a fun dessert.

100

Lil' Blueberry Angels

INGREDIENTS

1 (8-oz) package blueberries

1 cup simple syrup

1 cup Chambord

½ cup Grand Marnier

1 tsp granulated sugar

   Vanilla ice cream

   Individual angel food cakes

Serves at least 8

INSTRUCTIONS

Combine blueberries, simple syrup, Chambord, Grand Marnier, and sugar in a small saucepan. Bring to a boil and remain boiling for 5 minutes to reduce and thicken. Spoon vanilla ice cream on the angel food cake and drizzle reduction over top.

These individual sized pies are just the right amount of sweet after a delicious dinner. We top ours with Oreos or Twix but they are really good even just plain.

Mini Oreo Crème Pies

INGREDIENTS

1 14-oz can condensed milk
1 pint heavy cream
1 cup crushed oreos
   Graham cracker mini-crusts

Serves 8 (with plenty left for licking the bowl)

INSTRUCTIONS

Whip together milk, cream and crushed Oreos in a
Kitchen Aid. Pour into mini-crusts, garnish with your
favorite candy and chill in the refrigerator until serving.

*The girls hard at work behind the scenes styling and
shooting. Oreo day was a favorite since (of course!) we ate
all the creations each day. Pictured: Key grips, stylists and
photographer – Carlisle, Cristina, Cate, and Caroline.*

This is an elevated version of an old classic. Really easy to create as a pretty presentation too.

Whoopie Pie S'mores

How in the world can a whoopie pie get even better? Well, by creating your own personalized filling... that's how!

INGREDIENTS

1 15-oz package devil's food cake mix*
1 3.4-oz package instant vanilla pudding
3 eggs
½ cup vegetable oil
½ cup water
1 teaspoon vanilla extract
1 teaspoon cinnamon
   Chocolate chips
   Marshmallows
   Nutella & peanut butter!

Serves 8

*Devil's Food Cake is necessary – don't substitute the mix.

INSTRUCTIONS

Heat oven to 350 degrees. Combine all ingredients except marshmallows, Nutella, chocolate chips, and peanut butter. Mix until all the lumps are smooth.

Scoop batter onto wax paper using a small ice cream scooper. (I also spray the paper with Pam to keep it from sticking). Sprinkle top with chocolate chips. Bake for 12 minutes until a toothpick comes clean from the center.

Let cool. The 'whoopie pies' will be slightly puffy, cakey and the perfect soft crunch to build your S'more.

Invite your friends over for backyard drinks and dessert! Build an outdoor fire, toast up some marshmallows and then place between the two sides of whoopie pie cookies. For extra ah-mazing, spread Nutella or peanut butter on each side. Your friends will love you forever.

You can do this with any flavor ice cream and any favorite fruit but the combination of the caramel, watermelon and cinnamon has a creamy, fresh taste that is absolutely delicious.

Caramel Watermelon Ice Cream

PER SERVING

2   scoops of Dulce de Leche ice cream

Watermelon, cut in rectangles

Caramel sauce

Cinnamon sugar

INSTRUCTIONS

Scoop ice cream into bowl. Put caramel sauce in a
separate bowl. Dip watermelon chunks into caramel and
then sprinkle with cinnamon sugar. Put watermelon on
top of ice cream and top with more caramel.

*The flavor combination is out of this world.
No need to wait for bananas to ripen from the
store, this combination delivers a punch of flavor.*

Peanut Butter Banana Split Pudding

INGREDIENTS

1   package of banana pudding
    Whipped cream
    Reeses peanut butter cups

Serves 4

INSTRUCTIONS

Place 2 peanut butter cups in pudding dish. Make pudding mix according to package instructions. Pour over top of candy. Add whipped cream and peanut butter cup garnish.

Maine Squad loves our Ogunquit Restaurants!

Amore Breakfast
Angelina's Ristorante
Backyard
Bandito's Mexican Grill
Barnacle Billy's
Beach Basket
BeachFire Bar & Grille
Beachmere Blue Bistro
Bessie's
Black Boar Inn
Black Sushi
Bread & Roses
Brix & Brine
Caffe Prego
Charlie's Take Out
Clay Hill Farm
Coastal Wine
Cornerstone-Artisan Pizza
Cove Café
Crooked Pine
Egg & I

Five-O Shore Road
Food for Thought
Front Porch
Front Yard
Hook's Chill & Grill
Jackie's Too
Java Coffee & Tea
Jonathan's Restaurant
La Orilla Taps
La Pizzeria
Leavitt Theater Restaurant
Lobster Shack
Loveshack Juicery
Maine Street
MC Perkins Cove
Nikanos
Northern Union
Oarweed Restaurant
Ogunquit Beach Lobster House
Ogunquit House of Pizza
Ogunquit Lobster Pound

Old Village Inn
Patio 03907
Pizza Napoli
Raspberri's
Roberto's Italian
Rose Cove Café
Smokey B's
So Zap
Splash
Surf Point 360
That Place
The Greenery Cafe
The Omelette Factory
The Trap
Treehouse Taqueria
Village Market
West Meadow Pub
Wild Blueberry Café

THANK YOU!!!!!!!!!!!

My parents on Ogunquit Beach. 1965

This book is dedicated to my loving, caring parents who have always guided us to have fun, do good, and love each other unconditionally. And, thank you Mom/Noni for instilling the love of cooking and family gatherings.

CPSIA information can be obtained
at www.ICGtesting.com
Printed in the USA
LVHW070821070121
675963LV00007B/21

9 781735 818696